DIARY

OF A
MINECRAFT
CREEPER

Book 2

Silent but Deadly

by Pixel Kid and
Zack Zombie

Friday

Hssssss...

BOOM!

That was the scene at my homeroom class today.

It all started when Ms. Nilnose, our homeroom teacher, announced...

"In a few weeks, our class is going to put on a school play."

The class was silent for a few seconds.

But then it exploded.

Seriously...some of the Creeper kids exploded right then and there.

But not me.

This diary has been helping me work through my feelings, so I didn't combust.

At least not thisssss time.

Oh man, there goes my lisp again.

It always slipths out whenever I get nervous.

Anyway, it took Ms. Nilnose nearly five minutes to get the class settled down.

"But why do we need to do a school play?" asked a Ghast girl, wailing.

"The principal thinks it will be a great chance for our class and Mr. Grossegg's class to work together," Ms. Nilnose said. "It will be a great chance to make new friends."

Cool! My friend Harry is in Mr. Grossegg's homeroom class. It's going to be great to hang out with him, especially during all the drama.

Harry's a really cool guy. But he's got kind of a temper.

But Harry said that it's because he's part of the O'Brien clan from the Nether.

He said something about his family being full of hotheads. Especially when people make fun of their name.

Harry O'Brien. . .I don't get it.

Anyway, when I got home from school I told my parents what happened.

"Son, I am so proud that you kept it together," my dad said. "I kind of like having you around."

"Yes, dear. We heard about the unfortunate incident at school today," my mom said.

"So what caused the commotion in the first place?" asked Dad.

"Oh, Ms. Nilnose told us that we're going to be putting together a school play."

"Oh! Your Grandma Twilight will be so excited to hear this news! She used to be a great actress, you know. You have to tell her all about it when your grandparents come over this weekend," Mom said. "Oh, she'll be so excited, she'll talk your ears off!"

Wait. . .What?

Man, parents say some of the weirdest things sometimes.

Creepers don't even have ears. . .

Saturday

I was hanging out with the guys at our favorite spot today.

There's a forest biome just around the corner from my house that we've been going to since we were kids. We go there a lot when we want to talk about bro stuff.

"So, did your class get forced into doing a big project?" asked my buddy, Ed the Enderman.

"Jasper's class and my class got put together to do a school play," Harry said. "What about your class?"

"Our class combined with Ed's," said Ned the Wither.

"And we had to form groups and do a science project," continued Jed the Wither.

"And we have no idea what kind of project we're going to do." said Fred the Wither.

If you didn't know, Ned, Jed and Fred are a Wither. Or they are Withers. Or is it Witheren? Or. . .eh, forget it.

"Man, I wish we could do a play instead," sighed Ed. "It would be so much easier than a science project."

"At least you don't have to worry about stage fright," Harry said.

"You know, I had an uncle once who wanted to act," I said. "He used to work at a Zombie theatre. One day, the main actor was sick, so they asked my uncle to perform that day. My uncle got really excited because he finally got a chance to live out his dream."

"So what happened to him?"

"Let's just say, a new supermarket just opened up where the theatre used to be."

Sunday

My grandparents came to visit our house today. They live in another Biome, so we don't see them that often. So it's always nice when they come to visit.

My grandparents arrived at our house around dinnertime. Mom was cooking dinner and Dad was grocery shopping with Seymour, my little brother.

DING DONG!

"Jasper, can you please get the door?" shouted Mom from the kitchen.

I went and opened the door and. . .

"If it isn't our favorite grandson!" shouted Grandpa Major.

"Come over here, snoodkim," said Grandma Twilight as she gave me slobbery kiss.

Blech.

HONK HONK!

We turned around and saw my dad getting out of the car with my little brother. My grandparents rushed to play with my little brother, and I helped my dad with the bags from the shopping trip.

Yeah. . .I know what you're thinking.

But I'm really good at balancing stuff on my head.

As we went inside, the dining table was ready. And on the table was my favorite food. . .PUMPKIN PIE!

I was so excited that I zoned out from my family and purely focused on eating my pumpkin pie.

Mmmmm, pumpkin pie.

"Jasper. . .JASPER!" said my mom.

I looked up as everybody was staring at me gobble up the orange goodness.

"Aren't you going to tell your grandmother about your exciting new school project?" asked Mom.

"Oh, right! Grandma, we're doing a big play at school."

"That's delightful, Jasper! What play are you doing?

"Ummmm. . ."

"Oh, don't worry, dear," Grandma said. "Just remember, give it all you got and you'll be a smash."

Huh?

"Yes, I remember the days that we really brought the house down. . ."

Wait. . .What?

"We had some really blow out performances in my day. . ." Grandma said.

What in the. . .?

She just kept talking for a while. And the more she talked, the more scared I got. So, I just went back to eating my pumpkin pie.

But man, acting sounds like it could get a Creeper killed.

Later, I was about to go to sleep when there was a knock on my door.

The door slowly opened, and my parents popped their heads in.

"Hey, sweetie, are you about to go to bed?" asked my mom.

"We have a little present for you," my dad said.

"A present! What is it?"

"Well, after you bravely saved your class a few weeks ago, your father and I thought we would get you something you could use in case you find yourself in trouble again," my mom said with a smile.

Whoa, I wonder what it is?

Then the parents pulled out a huge box.

So I jumped out of my bed and ran to my door to see the gift that my parents got me.

My parents put the huge box on the floor.

Then I opened it.

It looked like a brick. . .with buttons.

"What is it?"

"Honey, it's the latest phone with all the gadgets," my mom said. "That's what the old lady at the supermarket said."

14

"And she said that it could also use it as a paperweight," my dad said.

Something tells me I should say goodbye to what's left of my social life. . .

Monday

I wasn't really sure how to feel about practicing our school play today.

I mean, my grandma made it sound like World War III with all those 'blow out audiences' and 'explosive performances' and stuff.

I'm just surprised how she could still crack a smile after all that destruction.

While we waited for class to start, I showed Harry my new phone.

"Whoa, Jasper," Harry said. "You can mine for diamonds with this thing."

"HAHAHAHA!" laughed a voice behind us. "What is THAT?"

We turned around to find a really tall and fat Creeper, laughing. There was also a Blaze, a Zombie, and a Slime snickering behind him.

"That's the lamest thing I have ever seen! laughed the big Creeper as he picked his nose and flicked it at me. Then he turned around and walked away with his gang. . .still laughing.

"Who was that?" I asked Harry.

"Don't worry about him, Jasper. That's just Burt Farkus; he's a real troublemaker," sighed Harry.

"Who?"

"Burt Farkus. He likes to bully some of the other kids at school. And he always travels around with his posse wherever he goes. There's Jeb the Blaze. . .he's a real hothead. There's Braden the Zombie, he's kind of gutless. And then there's Todd the

17

Slime. . .But, you've got to be careful around that guy. . .he's real slippery."

HSSSSSSS.

"Don't worry about them, Jasper. Just stay away from them and they won't bother you too much," Harry said.

But I wasn't sure whether to trust Harry or my bodily instincts.

HSSSSSSS.

"Jasper, just breathe."

PRRFT!

"Hello, class, my name is Ms. Moldini and I am your drama teacher. Today we will be working on your plays together. To begin, we will be forming smaller groups, so when I call out your name, please head to the area where your group will be."

Man, I hope I'm in the same group as Harry.

"Jasper Creeper and Harry O'Brien, head over to the left corner," Ms. Moldini said.

Harry and I high-fived each other as we walked to the corner. Well sort of. . .I always have a hard time getting my foot up that high.

"Burt, Jeb, Braden and Todd, please head over to the left corner with Jasper and Harry," continued Ms. Moldini.

HSSSSS.

I gave a glance at Harry to see what he was thinking about. But his eyes started glowing for some reason.

Tuesday

Today's drama class was worse than the first one.

Now, it didn't start out too bad.

But it ended in disaster.

"Each group will pick a different story to act out. It has to be based on Minecraft Lore that you have heard or read about," said Ms. Moldini.

Most of the class let out a sigh, but Harry and I high fived each other again. . .Well, sort of. . .

Anyway, Minecraft Lore is awesome. Harry and I even make up our own stories and create Minecraft maps that we spend all day playing. We would act out stories in our Bro Cave.

Like, some of our favorite stories are:

Thunder from Down Under

Attack of the Barking Spider

Breaking Wind

But our favorite story by far was one my dad told me called, 'Sir Farts-a-lot and the Ender Dragon.'

It's about a Creeper knight who had a Gold Sword and killed an Ender Dragon.

So epic!

Me and Harry were totally psyched about putting on our play now.

And this time, I can finally be Sir Farts-a-lot and slay the Ender Dragon.

That's because Harry's always plays Sir Farts-a-lot. He said something about being a better Sir Farts-a-lot because he has hands and stuff.

But, whatever, this time it's my turn.

So, we started working on the script.

But Burt and his gang were walking around the classroom making fun of the other kids and their plays.

HSSSSS.

Later, when we were busy writing our play, I smelled hot gunpowder breath on the back of my neck.

"SIR FARTS-A-LOT?!!!! Hey, guys, check this out," Burt said, grabbing my script.

"Hey!" I said.

Burt and his gang just laughed at us and made fun of our play.

"Dude, you can't even hold a sword," Jeb the Blaze said.

"You can't even ride a horse," Braden the Zombie said.

24

"He'll explode before he even gets near the Ender Dragon," Todd the Slime said.

"But he sure can fart a lot!" Burt said.

"HAHAHAHAHAHA!"

Then Ms. Moldini walked by to see how we were doing.

"How are you boys doing with your project?" she asked.

This was my time to show her our great script. I was gathering the papers and was about to get up, when all of a sudden Burt jumped in.

"We're going to do a play called Sir Farts-a-lot and the Ender Dragon," Burt said.

Ms. Moldini nodded and smiled. "That's a great idea, Burt! Who is playing who?"

"Well, I'm going play Sir Farts-a-lot because I'm a natural hero. Jeb will be my squire because he can light up the path in my adventures. Todd can be the Villager who gives me the Gold Sword, and Braden will be another Villager who tells me how to slay the Ender Dragon."

"Those are great ideas, Burt. And what will Jasper and Harry do?" asked Ms. Moldini.

"They're going to play the Ender Dragon!" exclaimed Burt.

Wait. . .What?

"That sounds nice, Burt," Ms. Moldini said. "I'm looking forward to seeing your play."

Harry and I just looked at each other.

Then Burt and his minions walked away laughing.

Man, talk about drama.

HSSSSSS.

Wednesday

Today at lunchtime, me and the guys just sat around the lunch table in silence.

Yeah, we were all having a bad day.

"Man, I thought this science project would be fun," said Ed the Enderman.

"Yeah, our school play is a mess too," grunted Harry.

Silence again at the table.

"So what's the science project you guys are working on?" I asked the others.

"We decided to do an experiment on Withers," Ned said.

"Yeah. We're going to test to see if we could separate ourselves into three separate mobs," said Jed.

"And then we want to see if we could combine at will," finished Fred.

"Whoa. That's crazy!"

"Yeah, I came up with the idea after we got creamed at dodge ball the other day," Ed said.

Wow. That sounded awesome! It would be really great to see that work.

All of a sudden. . .

"RAWWWRRRRRRRR!!!!"

"AHHHHH!!!"

PLOP!

"EWWWWWWW!" a bunch of kids in the cafeteria shrieked.

"Hahaha! Jasper, maybe we should call you Sir Drops-A-Lot," Burt said, high-fiving his guys.

HSSSSSSSSSSSS.

"Ah! He's gonna explode. . .run!" shouted Todd. And Burt and his gang ran off.

"Nice one, Jasper," Harry said.

After school, I went to the entrance of the mineshaft our class visited a few weeks ago.

Ever since we saved my class, my friend Steve and I have made that our regular hang out.

Steve's my human friend. He kind of reminds me of Harry, but with eyeballs.

None of the other guys have met him, though.

But I think that's a good thing.

I can only image how Ed, Ned, Jed, and Fred would react.

But the one I'm really concerned about is Harry. . .

Especially because something tells me that Harry and Steve might be related. . .but not in a good way.

Anyway, I was sitting near the mineshaft, still worried about the Burt situation.

HSSSSS.

"Whoa, Jasper, what's going on, buddy?" asked Steve looking worried.

I wasn't sure if he was worried about me. . .or worried about his life.

"Hey, Steve. I just had a rough day at school, thasss all," I sighed.

"What happened?"

"Well, we have this school play we need to put on, and I got put in the same group with a gang of bullies. Now they're bullying me and my friends."

"Oh, one of those, huh?" Steve said as he sat next to me.

"You know what, Jasper? I used to have a bully," Steve said.

"What? You? No way."

"Yeah, it was hard."

"So what did you do?"

"Well, me and the guy bullying me ended up becoming best friends," Steve said.

"No way! That's crazy!"

"Yeah, I found out that the reason he was bullying me so much was because somebody was bullying him," Steve said. "So, I decided I was going to help him out."

"Whoa."

Wow, Steve's got some guts.

Man, I wish I had guts.

But I don't think creepers have guts. If we did, I think they'd probably be in our feet.

"But, Steve, that sounds really hard," I said. "Like, how can I even start being nice to Burt and his goons? Every time I'm around them I feel like I'm going to explode."

"Well, Jasper, you're either going to be the hero, or you can get your revenge and before you know it, you end up becoming the villain," Steve said.

"Whoa, that's deep."

"You're welcome," Steve said.

"Oh, I almost forgot. I brought you a gift," I said and pushed the bag near my feet to Steve.

Steve opened the bag.

"Thanks, man, just what I needed! More gunpowder for my TNT! And there's so much here. You must've been working on this for days."

"Naw, last night was Burrito night at my house."

Thursday

This school play just seems to be getting worse every day.

Today, Ms. Nilnose announced that we're going to be performing our school play in front of our parents!

When the class heard that, it erupted into chaos.

Endermen were teleporting everywhere. Skeletons kids were falling apart. Zombie kids spilled their guts. And, of course, a lot of hissing came from Creeper kids.

Including me.

I really didn't want my parents coming to school. And I knew my grandparents would probably be coming too.

Man, I can imagine it now. I'm going to be on stage and everybody in the whole world is going to know what a wimp I am, especially when Burt and his minions step all over me.

SCREEEEEEEEEEEEEECH!

"OOOOOOOOOOOH!!!"

"Quiet down!" Ms. Nilnose yelled as she finished dragging her fingernails down the blackboard.

"The performance will be in two Saturdays' time. The school will provide the costumes for your characters, and Ms. Moldini will help you with rehearsals. Now off you go."

Then the class mumbled their way out of the classroom.

Like usual, Harry and I were the only ones in our group doing the work. I didn't even know where Burt and his gang were.

We made a list of the costumes and asked for some trees and a cave to be placed in the background. Once we finished, Ms. Moldini walked by and picked up our list.

She was giving nods of approval as she read down the list and then asked, "Where is the rest of your group?"

Harry and I looked at each other, scared.

"Um. . .I-I'm not sure, Ms. Moldini," I stuttered.

Just as Ms. Moldini was about to reply, Burt and his gang burst through the door.

Uh. Oh.

Then Ms. Moldini walked over and gave them "the talk."

Harry and just I looked at each other.

Yeah. . .we're doomed.

Then Burt and his goons slowly crept over in our direction.

HSSSSSS.

"So, you ratted on us, heh?" fumed Burt.

Jeb, Braden, and Todd just stood behind him with angry looks on their faces.

"I. . .I. . .just told her you were outside, thasssss all. . ." I said nervously.

"We didn't rat on you," Harry said. "You just didn't come to class and Ms. Moldini noticed."

Yeah, we're dead.

You know, Harry is a great friend. . .but sometimes he doesn't know when to be scared.

"Oh, is that what happened?" snapped Burt. "Well why don't you shut your pie hole. . .HEROBRINE!"

"What did you call me?" asked Harry.

Oh, boy. Now Burt did it.

That's the one name Harry hates being called.

Nobody knows why, really.

Me and the guys tried to look it up. But all we found out was that in Harry's native language it means 'boy with face like butt'. . .or something like that."

But man, Harry just goes ballistic every time somebody says it.

"HE-RO-BRINE! HE-RO-BRINE! HE-RO-BRINE!" taunted Burt.

Suddenly, things in the classroom started to heat up.

40

I took a quick glance and knew Burt and his gang were in deep trouble. . .and so were the rest of us.

If you didn't know, Harry started going through some weird changes since he started going through puberty.

All I know, is that there was a fire truck in front of his house like three days this week.

All of sudden, Harry's eyes started glowing and then smoke started coming out his eyes. . .and ears, I think.

Next thing you know. . .

ZZZZZZZT!

KABAAAAAMMMMMM!

Burt managed to react quickly and dodged the blast. But the wall and curtains behind Burt weren't so lucky. . .

Next thing we knew, all the mob kids were running and screaming and everybody rushed out of the drama classroom.

We saw Burt and his friends outside huddled and fake crying as Ms. Moldini was talking to them.

Harry and I stood together outside and watched as the drama classroom burned down.

"Oh my gosh. . .was that me?" whispered Harry.

"Harry and Jasper," seethed Ms. Moldini.

Harry and I turned our heads slowly to her.

It seemed our end would come in a different way. . .

"Go to the principal's office. . .RIGHT NOW!"

Friday

So, yesterday...oh, man, yesterday.

That was BAD!

Man, I'm about to explode just thinking about it.

After the whole drama room went up in flames, Harry and I were ordered to the principal's office.

We sat quietly next to each other and dreaded when the door opened. Because through them came our parents.

My parents were hissing.

And the O'Brien's definitely raised the temperature of the room.

Both our parents gave us a quadruple dose of the "I'm not mad, just disappointed" killer stares as they were ushered inside the office.

Oh boy. We were in deep, DEEP trouble.

After the longest thirty minutes ever, our parents finally came out.

"Thank you, Principal Shortsnout, we'll be sure to pass the advice you gave us to Jasper," I heard my dad say.

Goodbye, Harriet. Goodbye, Harold," my mom said to the O'Brien's.

Harry and I gave each other a look, which was probably the last time we were ever going to see each other.

"Come on, Jasper. We're going home," said my dad in a really disappointed voice.

HSSSSS.

"What were you thinking?" my dad said, scolding me in the car.

"Honey, why would you be so mean to such a nice boy like Burt Farkus?" asked my mom.

Oh man, Burt must have told them it was our fault! I thought.

That would explain why he didn't get in trouble.

"Jasper, you've been suspended from school for the rest of the day, and the principal suggested that you take that time to reflect on your actions."

As the car pulled into the driveway to our house, I got out and went to my room.

At night, I went to see my mom in the kitchen to see if I could explain the situation.

I wasn't too hopeful though.

Yeah, adults never listen to a kid's side of the story.

It's like when the adults get together, all we kids can do is wear our striped jumpsuits and wait in our cells until our sentence is over.

"Honey, your father and I are really worried about you. We thought you finally settled into your new school and then you go and set your drama classroom on fire."

"Mom. I didn't want that to happen! It's just that. . ."

"My goodness, do you know how many kids could've gotten hurt?" she said as she started hissing.

Uh-oh. Mom hissing. Bad sign. Really bad sign.

That's because my mom works as a secretary in a powerplant.

Who knows what she's been exposed to at that place.

So, in order not have to explain to my dad why my mom went nuclear, I jumped in and interrupted my mom and blurted out the whole story.

"Well, why didn't you say anything earlier?" Mom asked.

I just sat there quiet for a while.

Then she gave me a hug.

...Or, whatever a hug without hands is called.

Yeah. . . needed that.

Later, I heard a knock on my door. The door opened, and my dad's head popped in.

"Hey, champ," he said.

Oh man, I hope Mom told him what really happened.

"I'm sorry for blowing up at you yesterday," my dad said.

Wait. . .What?

"It was very brave of you to tell your mother about what really happened," my dad said. "I know parents don't always listen sometimes."

Whoa. Did he just say that?

"And I heard about the bullies," my dad continued. "Yeah, bullies are really tough to deal with. Especially when they call you

49

names or when they throw cactus at you, and when they lock you in the janitor's closet. . .and especially the wedgies, those are really painful."

Huh?

"But no matter what, son, don't let them get to you. You just keep being the great little kid that you are, okay?"

"Uh. . .sure, Dad."

And with that, Dad patted me on the head and went down to help Mom with dinner.

You know, parents can be pretty weird sometimes.

But, you know. . .sometimes they can be really awesome too.

Saturday

Today, Harry came over to my house to work on the school play.

We worked on our script for a while, until we realized it would be much more fun to play video games instead.

"I really don't think Burt and his gang are going to help us with this play," Harry said, rolling his eyes.

Or I think he did.

Yeah, Harry kinda falls short on the eyeball department.

Anyway, despite the stress at school, I really think our play is going is going to be great.

The story goes like this:

Sir Farts-a-lot is sent on a quest to defeat the Ender Dragon that is terrorising a small town. The Village Elders gift him a Gold Sword and send him off to defeat the Ender Dragon. After an epic battle, Sir Farts-a-lot wins and takes the Ender Dragon's Egg back to the village and makes a huge omelette.

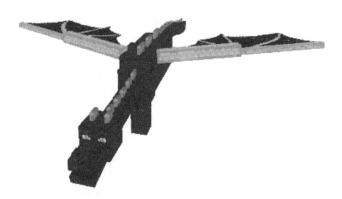

"Hey, Jasper, how's Sir Farts-a-lot gonna defeat the Ender Dragon?" Harry asked. "I mean, using the Gold Sword is kinda old school."

"Hey, why don't we add a plot twist," I said. "Like he could use balloon fart bombs."

"Yeah, we can even make it really scary," Harry said. "Like make the Enderdragon rip Sir Farts-a-lots arms off."

"Uh. . .we can't make it too scary," I said. "I really don't want to have to move to a new school again."

We just looked at each other.

"HSSSSS. . .BOOM!" Harry said.

Then we just burst out laughing.

Later, to help me feel better, Mom made me one of my favorite foods in the whole Overworld. . .

CAKE!

While we were eating dessert, Dad asked about the school play. So I told him about the story we had so far.

"That's lame," my sister Ima said. "Everyone knows that story."

"Well ours is going to be different. . .You'll see."

"Why don't you talk to Grandma Ada?" my dad said. "I remember her saying she had seen an Ender Dragon once."

"WHAT? Grandma Ada saw a real Ender Dragon?"

You know, that would explain her color change.

Man, grandmas got it hard.

Wow, mad props to all the old ladies.

Sunday

I was really excited to see my other grandparents today.

On our way there, my little brother fell asleep in his car seat, so we kept real quiet.

They say you shouldn't wake a baby creeper while he's sleeping.

My uncle tried waking a baby Creeper once.

They had to rush him to the hospital.

It took them six hours to just to dig the rattle out of his nose.

But they never did find the binky.

Grandma Ada had prepared a feast for us when we arrived.

I love eating at Grandma Ada's. She makes the best mushroom stew.

After our ginormous lunch, me and my sister Ima went to explore Grandma and Grandpa's house.

Ima and I used to play Hide and Sneak when we used to visit our grandparents.

Ima was really good too. . .

As for me, let's just say grandma got used to cleaning the little piles of gunpowder around the house.

One time, Ima hid in the library and pretended to be a part of the wall.

All I remember is that when she jumped out, everything went black.

Later, my dad said we had enough gunpowder to make fireworks for weeks.

So, I asked Ima if she wanted to play a game of Hide and Sneak.

But she said she was too cool for a "kiddy" game like that.

Wow. . .that's cold.

Anyway, we decided to explore my grandma's collection of library books instead.

She's collected every book she's ever read since she was a baby Creeper.

Then Ima found a book that looked Enchanted.

"Whoa. . .what's that?" I asked.

"Looks like an Enchanted Book," Ima said, opening it up.

Inside, instead of enchantments, we found a bunch of old Minecraft stories.

As we were flipping the pages, I thought the pictures and fancy letters looked really cool.

All of a sudden, I saw the words, "The Legend of Sir Farts-a-lot" flash by.

"Hey, wait a minute!" I said as I grabbed the book from Ima and started flipping back to the pages to find the Sir Farts-a-lot story.

Man, I thought Dad made up this story. But it's actually true? Whoa!

So, I started reading. . .

Once upon a time, there was a young Creeper boy named Farts-a-lot. He wasn't the strongest creeper in the village, or the smartest.

But he did fart, a lot.

One day, his village was being attacked. And when Farts-a-lot saw the purple clouds of smoke in the sky, he knew that the Ender Dragon was responsible.

Everything was in chaos. So, little Farts-a-lot decided he was going to help.

But how could a small Creeper like him take down the legendary Ender Dragon?

So, he ran to the ancient village library and started to read more about the Ender Dragon.

And after reading a lot of books, he finally found the Ender Dragon's weakness. He would have to slay the Ender Dragon with a Golden sword.

Then he ran to the Villagers and told them his plan. . .but they laughed at him.

"You can't even hold a sword," one Creeper said.

"You can't even ride a horse," another Creeper said.

"He'll explode before he even gets near the Ender Dragon," a bunch of other Creeper villagers said.

But the little creeper didn't let that stop him because he knew his plan would work.

So, Farts-a-lot grabbed his dad's Golden Sword and decided to make a journey to the lair of the Ender Dragon.

After traveling for a few days, he found the lair of the Ender Dragon but the Ender Dragon wasn't there. So, Farts-a-lot decided to wait until dark to put his plan into action.

Meanwhile, he lit some torches to keep himself warm. But, as it grew dark, suddenly the light from the fires attracted the Ender Dragon.

"RAAAAAARRRRRRRR! WHO GOES THERE? RAAAAAARRRRRRRR!" the Ender Dragon roared.

The little Creeper was surprised and went to grab the Golden Sword.

But no matter how hard he tried, he couldn't get a good grip.

"RAAAAAARRRRRRRR! the Ender Dragon roared as it got closer.

Oh no! Maybe the other Creeper Villagers were right. Maybe this was a fool's quest.

"RAAAAAARRRRRRRR! the Ender Dragon roared again and was almost upon the little Creeper.

And just when the Ender Dragon was close enough to eat the little Creeper. . .

"RAAAAAARRRRRRRR!

PRRFFT.

BOOOOOOOOOOOOOOOOOOOOOM!

A huge fireball blasted the Ender Dragon so hard that it sent him to the moon.

And when the little Creeper opened his eyes. . .

Bop!

A Dragon Egg dropped right next to him.

Farts-a-lot took the Dragon Egg back to the village. And all the Villagers were so amazed by his bravery, they decided to knight him.

And from then on, he was known as Sir Farts-A-Lot—Knight of All that is Silent, but Deadly.

And they all celebrated with a nice omelette dinner.

Whoa, so that's the whole story of Sir Farts-a-lot!

Man, this is better than I thought.

"Oh, I see you've found my favorite Minecraft storybook," piped Grandma Ada.

Ima and I turned around to find our grandma at the door.

"Sorry for being nosy, Grandma. We just haven't visited the library in a while," Ima said.

"This is totally different than the story I heard about Sir Farts-a-lot," I said.

"Of course, it is! It's based on our family's history with the Ender Dragon," Grandma Ada said.

"Whoa!"

"Grandma, do you think I can use this story for my school play?" I asked.

"Fart away, young one. Go and save the Overworld from the Ender Dragon," Grandma Ada said with a smile.

Man, I was so excited.

We're gonna have the best play in the whole school.

And it's going to totally bring the house down.

Wait. . .what did I just say?

Monday

Today was Harry and my first day back after getting in trouble.

So when I entered my homeroom, everything went crazy.

I guess they still thought Harry and I destroyed the drama room.

Either that, or they were serving mystery Zombie meat in the cafeteria again today.

Anyway, as I was walking toward my English class, I rounded a corner in the hallway.

Suddenly...

"RAWWWWR!"

"AHHH!"

PLOP.

"Hahaha!" Burt laughed. "Look, guys, Sir Drops-a-lot is afraid of his own shadow!"

"Hahaha!" roared Jeb the Blaze.

"Hahaha!" roared Todd the Slime.

"Urgh," moaned Braden the Zombie.

As Burt and his gang walked away laughing, I started to shuffle my feet to hide my little accident.

Man, maybe I should drop out of school and become a fireworks salesman.

I can imagine it now. . .

"Hey, would you like to buy some fireworkssssss?"

Tuesday

Today, we had to do some rehearsals for our performance on Saturday.

Ms. Moldini even managed to get the costumes that we asked for.

I hate to admit it, but Burt did look really cool in his Sir Farts-a-lot costume.

But Harry and I had to squeeze into a really small Ender Dragon outfit.

And, of course, I got the back end of the job.

Yup, I was the Ender butt.

Harry and I printed out extra copies of the new script and gave them to Burt and his gang to read.

"What? Why does Sir Farts-a-lot not have a Gold Sword?" shouted Burt.

"Yeah, and why does he read books?" asked Todd.

"*Urgh. . .*" grunted Braden.

"Well, Ms. Moldini said we can make our own unique version, so that's what me and Jasper did," Harry said.

"But you made Sir Farts-a-lot lame," said Jeb.

"Yeah, this is not what we signed up for. Come on, gang, let's just do our own thing," Burt said while strutting away and swinging his sword.

HSSSS.

After class, I went to go see Steve.

He wasn't at our usual spot, so I just sat down on the ground and waited.

. . .and then my eye sockets started tearing up.

"Whoa, Jasper. You're crying so hard, I can almost tell what you had for breakfast," said Steve.

I turned around and I saw Steve coming out of the mineshaft.

He did a quick glance at me and said, "You know what? I want to show you something."

We walked for a while until we finally got to the Forest Biome. He climbed up to the top of a big hill and I followed him.

Once we go to the top, we sat down. I looked ahead and wow. . .the view was awesome.

"So, what's eating you, Jasper?" asked Steve.

Wait. . .What?

"It's that bully again, right?"

"Yeah," I said, looking at my stubby feet.

"Well, Jasper, just remember that whatever this bully is doing to you, it's not your fault. From what I know, bullies only do those things because they're scared," said Steve.

Huh?

Burt scared? That sounded weird.

"Really?" I asked.

"Yeah. I think every kid in school is scared, but especially the bullies. They try to make themselves feel better by picking on the other kids."

Whoa. That was deep. I can always count on Steve to impart some wisdom on me.

. . .But for some reason I always have a headache after.

"Thanks, Steve. I'll have think about that one," I said with a half-smile.

"There you go, that's the Jasper I know. Oh, and hey, you don't have any more gunpowder on you? I need it for some more TNT," Steve said.

"I kinda had a gunpowder buffet before you got here," I said. "Enjoy."

Wednesday

Today at lunch, Ed, Ned, Jed and Fred had some good news to share.

"We're totally making progress on our science project," said Ed the Enderman.

"From our experiments, it seems like different things cause different Wither reactions," Ed explained.

"Like, one test we tried," Ned said, "I ate a very spicy chilli. I felt it first, Jed felt it second, and Fred got the bubble guts.

"But we can't get to the next part of the experiment, though. Every time we try, Fred's butt goes nuclear," said Ed.

"Talk about explosive diarrhea. . ." whispered Ned.

"A dishonorable discharge. . ." said Jed.

"Here it comes again!" said Fred.

Then we all ran for cover.

Man, it's good to see my friends are having success with their project.

But, when are me and Harry going to resolve our drama class. . .drama?

Thursday

I totally wanted to skip school today.

But it's not like Creepers can fake going to school.

I mean, like if I try to fake a sneeze, I'll explode.

Or if I try to fake a cough, I'll explode.

And if I try to fake a fever, I'll explode.

Yeah, being a Creeper is no fun sometimes.

In drama class, Harry and I were trying to rehearse our play, but Burt and his gang were messing around again.

They would just run around with their fake swords and attack each other.

I was a bit creeped out when Braden the Zombie pulled of his arm and used it as a sword, though.

That was just wrong on so many levels.

Ms. Moldini came over and checked in on our practice.

"How's everything going?" she asked Harry. I'm sure she would have asked me if I was the front of the costume.

"Terrible!" Harry said. "Burt and his friends aren't helping us at all."

Oh man. . .

Then Ms. Moldini marched Burt and his gang toward us.

"All right, Jasper, I want to hear your side of this," said Ms. Moldini as I popped my head out of my Ender butt costume.

I looked over at Burt and his gang and they were giving me death stares.

But even though I was doomed, I took a deep breath and decided to tell the truth.

"Harry and I having been working on this script all week. But Burt, Jeb, Braden, and Todd haven't helped us one bit."

Ms. Moldini shook her head and turned to Burt and his friends.

"Burt, Jeb, Braden and Todd, please stop lollygagging and work with your group," said Ms. Moldini. Then she walked away to talk to the next group.

Gulp.

Harry and I both felt holes burning in the back of our heads. We turned around and saw Burt and his gang. . .and they were furious.

PRRRFT.

Now that Ms. Moldini is gone, you're going to get yours," scoffed Burt.

"You've done it now, runt," fumed Jeb.

"No one to protect you now..." breathed Todd.

"Urrrggghhh!" grunted Braden.

HSSSSSSSSSS.

"Run! He's gonna blow!" shouted Burt.

Then Burt and his guys, and the rest of the class, ran out of the room.

"But we'll see you tomorrow after school," Burt yelled as he ran out of the classroom. "That is if you're brave enough to meet us."

"WE'LL BE THERE!" Harry shouted way too loudly.

Harry and I stood there in silence.

Oh boy. What have we gotten ourselves into?

Friday

Today was the day.

Today was the day that I had to prove that I'm not a chicken.

HSSSSSSS. Cluck...Cluck.

Ed, Ned, Jed, and Fred decided to come along.

"We'll be here to back you up," they said together.

Man, I have some of the best friends.

Even though Fred still had the bubble guts.

Nasty.

So, we met Burt in the forest, a few miles away from the school.

Burt and his gang were already there.

And as we walked toward each other, it felt like we were in a Desert Biome Western.

Anyway, without saying a word, my friends and I walked toward Burt and his gang to what was probably going to be our doom.

We looked around and there were giant trees and an open space for us to stand. And behind the trees, there was a giant cave.

"So, squirt. You have two choices," Burt said. "Me and my boys can give you a severe beating or you can take a dare. What's it going to be?"

Now, even though Harry can shoot lasers from his eyes...

And even though Ed can teleport...

And even though Ned, Jed, and Fred had the dirty dynamite...

The truth was, we're just a bunch of kids.

We haven't even finished going through puberty yet.

But Burt and his goons? I think they've gone through puberty twice. That's probably why they're are a lot bigger and meaner than we are.

It's like they were born to pillage.

"The dare?" I said hesitantly.

"I thought so, pipsqueak. Then this is what you need to do," boomed Burt. "See that giant cave over there? Well you need to walk around inside for five minutes."

Heh, that didn't seem so bad.

"And you can't come out no matter what you hear or what you see," Burt said with a scary smile.

Wait. . .What?

I turned toward the cave and my friends gathered around me. I could hear Burt and his gang laugh and make bets on how long I'd stay in the cave.

HSSSSS.

"Jasper, keep it cool. It's just a cave! You can do this," encouraged Ed.

"Yeah, go Jasper!" cheered on Ned, Jed, and Fred.

I felt a hot, sweaty hand on my shoulder. "You've got this, dude," said Harry.

Nodding at my friends, I turned around and walked toward the cave.

HSSSSS.

It had been just over four minutes and nothing bad happened.

I'm gonna make it! I thought.

The cave was kind of peaceful, even though it was really dark and there was the occasional howling wind.

I started thinking of all the things that had happened to me these past few weeks.

The school play, the bullying, and all the drama.

But hopefully, I thought, maybe this dare will stop Burt and his minions from bullying me and my friends ever again.

Then suddenly. . .

RAAAWWWWRRRRR!

What in the world was that?!!!!!

HSSSSS.

The roar definitely came from inside the cave. So I started hopping out toward the opening.

"You're so close, Jasper! Just stay in the cave for another thirty seconds!" Harry shouted when he saw my head pop out.

Before I could reply, another roar echoed from the cave.

RAAAWWWWRRRRR!

PRRFFFFT.

Oh man, I just couldn't take it anymore. Either the roaring was going to get to me or being stuck in an enclosed space with my nervous stomach was going to do me in.

"Ten. . .Nine. . .Eight!"

RAAAWWWWRRRRR!

Oh man! The sound was getting louder!

"Seven. . .Six. . .Five!"

RAAAWWWWRRRRR!

"Four. . .Three. . .Two!"

"GRRRRAAAWWWWWWLLLLLL!!!!!!"

"AAAAAAHHHHHHHH!!!!

I couldn't take it anymore! I ran out of there like a bat out of the Nether.

Then right behind me. . .

"GRRRRAAAWWWWWWLLLLLL!!!!!!"

"LOOK OUT!"

As I dove to the ground, a huge beast came flying out of the cave.

"IT'S THE ENDER DRAGON!"

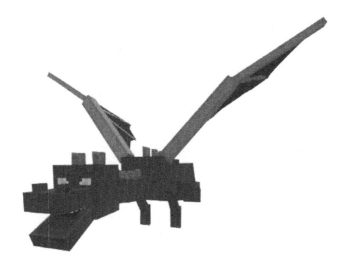

"WHAT THE CRAZY WHAT?!" yelled Harry as we ran toward the trees.

"Maybe there was a glitch and a Portal opened?" asked Ed.

We all hid in behind a tree and looked out in awe.

HSSSSSSS.

"Keep quiet, Jasper," whispered Ned, Jed, and Fred.

"It's not me!" I said. Then we looked over to the only other Creeper among us.

Burt was scared. And so were the rest of his minions.

"How did the Ender Dragon get out of the End?" Harry asked.

Then Burt's minions gave him up.

"It was Burt!" Braden said. "He wanted to fix you good, so he made an End portal in the cave hoping that you would fall through it."

"Seriously?!!!" Harry said as his eyes started glowing.

Well, whether it was the embarrassment of getting ousted by his friends, or Harry's glowing eyes, or the fact that we were all were sitting in a cloud of toxic air. . .sorry. . .

Burt just ran out into the field crying.

"WWWAAAAAAHHHHH!!!"

So there Burt was, in the middle of the open field, crying and hissing. . .But by then, the Ender Dragon saw him and came swooping back. . .and diving straight toward Burt.

We all gasped.

I couldn't leave Burt out there. No matter how mean he was to me.

I mean, he didn't deserve to get eaten by the Ender Dragon, right?

That was when I realized what I needed to do.

It's hero time!

Friday Later
that Night

"Everybody grab some branches!" I yelled.

So all the guys started breaking branches until we had enough to make some torches for each of us.

"All right, light them up!"

Jeb, the Blaze, and Harry lit them up.

We all grabbed a torch and ran toward the open area, to the other side of where Burt was.

"We started waving the torches like crazy mobs until we got the Ender Dragon's attention.

So instead of eating Burt, he now started heading to eat us.

"I hope you know what you're doing, Jasper!" Harry said. "Cause we are about to have some company!"

"Hold!" I said.

"Jasper, he's coming right at us!" Ed said.

"Hold!"

"He's crazy!" Ned said.

"He's nuts!" Jed said.

"He's inhaled too many toxic fumes!" Fred said.

"Hold!"

Gulp!

"NOOOOOOWWWWW!!!!"

Suddenly, we all threw our torches in the air, right when the Ender Dragon was going to chomp down on us.

PPRRRFFTT!

BOOOOOOOOOOOMMMMMMMMM!!!!

A giant fireball formed that hit the Ender Dragon dead on.

The force from the blast was so strong it blew us all back and blew some trees out of the ground behind us.

We thought we were dead, but then we all started getting up one by one.

"Where's the Ender Dragon?" Harry asked.

"LOOK!" Ed said, pointing to the moon.

As we all looked up, all we could see was a little speck on the moon flying around like a bug flying around a big piece of cheese.

"YEAAAAAAAAHHHHH!!!!!!"

All of us were jumping, screaming and giving high fives. Well. . .most of us.

"Where's Burt?" Harry asked.

Then as we looked around, we saw some leaves shivering in a far corner.

As we removed them, there was Burt under all the leaves. He had his thumb in his mouth and was rocking back and forth.

"Mommy, Mommy, Mommy, Mommy, Mommy!" Burt said.

"Well, so much for brave Sir Farts-a-lot," Harry said.

"Yeah, that guy's a real lion," Ed said sarcastically.

"Seems more like a chicken to me," Ned, Jed, and Fred said.

"What a loser," Jeb, Braden, and Todd said.

Right then, I remembered what Steve told me.

And I realized, it was decision time.

Was I going to kick Burt while he was down and become the villain?

You know, I thought. *Sweet revenge would taste really good right now.*

Or was I going to stand up and be the hero?

Well, I might not be a hero, but I knew what Sir Farts-a-lot, Knight of all that is Silent but Deadly would do.

Let's do this!

"Hey, guys, leave him alone. He was just scared like the rest of us," I said.

Then we all looked at each other.

"All right, man," Harry said, reaching out his hand to Burt.

"Thankssssss," Burt said with a surprisingly noticeable lisp.

Saturday

So yesterday, we survived getting eaten by the Ender Dragon.

And you'd think that was the scariest thing ever.

But today I'm really scared.

Because its performance day!

And I don't know how we're going to do because we barely had any rehearsals.

So, when we arrived at the hall, my family got ushered in to take their seats.

But I went backstage with the rest of the drama students.

I was curious to see how many people were in the audience because it sounded really noisy and crowded. So I poked my head out...

HSSSS!

"Hey, Jasper, calm down," said a voice behind me.

"Yeah, don't start hissing or I will too!"

I turned around and it was an Ender Dragon!

But then out from the Ender Dragon popped Burt and Jeb the Blaze.

Yeah, why they put a Blaze in that costume, I don't know, I thought. *I just felt really sorry for Burt.*

"Wow, that thing seems so real" I said. "I almost peed my pants."

"Hey, Jasper. I've been thinking," Burt said. "Since you really helped me out yesterday, I thought I could repay the favor."

"Yeah, thanks for saving us, man," chirped in Braden, Todd, and Jeb.

"We remembered that you always wanted to be Sir Farts-a-lot. . ." Burt said.

Then Harry came out dressed as Sir Farts-a-lot's squire and holding the Sir Farts-a-lot costume.

"Jasper, you know the play inside and out," Harry said. "You will be the best Sir Farts-a-lot the Overworld has ever seen."

"Yeah!" the other guys cheered.

"Guys, I don't know what to say. I'm just really happy that. . ."

"All right, Sir Farts-a-lot team, you guys are up next!" yelled Ms. Moldini.

PRFFFFT.

Sunday

Wow, yesterday was awesome!

I'm not going to lie.

The play was off the hook!

The other kids decorated the stage with a huge cave and some trees.

Braden the Zombie and Todd the Slime were Villagers—Ms. Moldini found them really realistic masks with huge noses.

Burt and Jeb roared onto the stage as the ferocious Ender Dragon. . .Oooh! So Creepy.

And I got on stage in my costume with my trustworthy squire, Harry.

And then, I remember the applause.

When we finished, Braden and Todd took their masks off and bowed.

Harry went to help Burt and Jeb out of the Ender Dragon costume and they bowed at the front of the stage.

Good thing too. Burt was kinda nervous, which meant serious warm air in Jeb's face.

And then I came out and took a bow.

Boy, the applause was amazing.

I looked into the crowd and saw huge cheesy grins on my parents' and grandparents' faces.

While my sister Ima was there folding her arms and rolling her eye sockets.

Though I think I caught her smiling. . .for like a second.

But me? I couldn't have been happier.

Thasss because I was happy that I wasn't being bullied anymore.

And I was happy that I ended with a new group of friends.

And I was happy that I didn't get eaten by the Ender Dragon.

But most of all, I was happy that I got to play my new favorite hero, Sir Farts-a-lot, and make him proud.

Yup, it's been an interesting couple of weeks.

But standing up there next to all my new friends, in front of my family, and making it through the adventure of a lifetime, I can honestly say. . .

. . .it was totally worth it.

THE END

Find out What
Happens Next in...

Diary of a Minecraft Creeper Book 3

Coming soon. . .

If you really liked this book, please tell a friend. I'm sure they will be happy you told them about it.

Leave Us a Review Too

Please support us by leaving a review. The more reviews we get the more books we will write!